CORRIDOR

Also by Saskia Hamilton

Poetry

As for Dream

Divide These

Canal

Editor

The Letters of Robert Lowell

Words in Air:
The Complete Correspondence between
Elizabeth Bishop and Robert Lowell

CORRIDOR

poems

Saskia Hamilton

Graywolf Press

This publication is made possible, in part, by the voters of Minnesota through a Minnesota State Arts Board Operating Support grant, thanks to a legislative appropriation from the arts and cultural heritage fund, and through grants from the National Endowment for the Arts and the Wells Fargo Foundation Minnesota. Significant support has also been provided by Target, the McKnight Foundation, Amazon.com, and other generous contributions from foundations, corporations, and individuals. To these organizations and individuals we offer our heartfelt thanks.

Published by Graywolf Press
250 Third Avenue North, Suite 600
Minneapolis, Minnesota 55401

www.graywolfpress.org

Published in the United States of America

ISBN 978-1-55597-675-0

2 4 6 8 9 7 5 3 1
First Graywolf Printing, 2014

Library of Congress Control Number: 2013958007

Cover design: Jeenee Lee Design

Cover art: Vilhelm Hammershøi, *Street in London*. Photo by Ole Haupt. Courtesy of Ny Carlsberg Glyptotek, Copenhagen.

Contents

I

Night-Jar — 5
Thaon — 6
Spiral — 7
Messenger — 8
Fare Forward — 9
Flatlands — 10
In the Fall — 11
Suspension — 12
Compass — 13
Inroads — 14
Flatlands — 15
Classical Experiment — 16

II

Once — 19
Rain Begins — 20
From a Letter — 21
Increase — 22
En Face — 23
Wintered — 24
House Tour — 26
To Admit — 27
Ivor Gurney — 28
Whorls by Bike-Lamp — 29
Concertgebouw — 30
Asleep Awake — 31
Disuse — 32

Apartments – 33
On. On. Stop. Stop. – 34
Leave – 35
Open Country – 36
Photograph: Paestum, c. 1860, Anonymous – 37
II to III – 38
On the Ground – 39

III

In the Corridor – 43
Men and Sheep – 45
Zwijgen – 46
Cover – 47
Milk Street – 48
Summered – 49
An Essay on Total Colony Collapse – 52
An Essay on Perspective – 53
Eaves – 54
Field Experiments – 55
Faring – 61
Night-Jar – 62

After *Gewritu secgað* – 65

Notes & Acknowledgments – 67

For Lucien, you see

CORRIDOR

I

Night-Jar

Hawking for moths at dusk: the night-jar
in the fen near the worn stone markers
of the old bishopric: ceded
to sentries of the forest: thence their fall,
one by one: thence centuries under-
foot of branch and brush and peat. Near us,
but where, it's gone: past the rides.

Thaon

In the first field, a man turns the hay.
Where there's ricks there's gates—six;
sufficient to the sojourner,

to the day. We parked by the fourth field
and descended the path cut by rain water
through fern, bark, and sticks. Litter of old
walls where the forest encroached on dwelling.

Down in the church named for the saint named
for stone, the villagers of Thanatos,
packed in, lie below the lifted floor, feet
pointed tentatively at the chancel.

Tarp covers their teeth and jaws.
Lichen and mold blue the grinning lion,
fish and worm, and outside, in the uncleared
valley, dandelion and poppies seed.

Unto the hour sufficient.
The long late one begins in the wood.
The bird's call seems to turn though it is
still in its bracken. Its round eye, somewhere

in there, takes in the dark
under the blackening
canopy of branches. Reversal, portal.

Spiral

Rows of pines, planted years ago—so many,
were you to count them on your fingers, you
would give up past a hundred span; and pain
doesn't yet know about it, while lording

over all other feeling. I'll explain these things
some day. In the meantime, rows
of pines, the quincunx pattern lost
in spirals and thickets of lesser branches

increasing their reach inexorably. The man
spoke of the bees: move the hive five miles
and they'll find their way; move it five feet,

and they'll die of confounding. A stacking
of three green boxes in the clearing,
the numbers buzzing among the numbers.

Messenger

Blackthorn had leafed out, and at the wood's edge,
muguet in the leaf litter. In the pasture,
the cattle, cropping grass, stepped sideways,
and the donkey turned its right ear,
then its left, as he approached. But he
had nothing earthly to say.

Fare Forward

Midsummer rain; then again. Numbering
the days. Then forty more of heavy air.
They arrange the order of the internal

forest of hours in our absence.
The numbers fall short.
In the shelter of the ruin, faces stare out

of five leafy capitals. They do not speak
their alarm: the donkey's ears round
the bending road to Egypt; the angel falls

head-first into the virgin's womb.
Inside their mouths of stone, do the dead yield?
The tractor turns its giant forks

to the field. Seed-sorter, seed-fixer, sacked;
petrochemicals, bodies, the gut: time
to build a hospital for travelers.

Flatlands

Horses and geese in a sodden field.
Solitaries with luggage on a wet platform.
Postage-stamp house on a bit of land,
a copse, a fold, a quadrant of wood,
lines of beech, lines of poplar,
miniature commentary magnified
in the glass, winter streaking the window,
the train bearing, not bearing the weight
within. Let this not be thought
(one thought to oneself), non-
thoughts of passengers on the way forward
backward through the hour.

In the Fall

"You're not going in there—?"
I turned but there was no passage,
only waking.

–

Dogs prostrate under the table, mud
dry on their flanks.
Milk in the pan of onions.

–

The change to schist along that road,
earth in the broken asphalt, gates or doors,
mainverblessness, lapidary
bees in the walls, stones fallen short
of the swollen stream north from where
it joins the sea and crosses my mouth.

–

In the bookshop, at the counter, the man
at the register adds up the cost, and you,
"Don't you want Apollinaire's letters?
You with your French tongue—" And *Minor Poets
of the Caroline Period* (3 vols.).

–

What to think of while all the while thinking
only of your hand thinking.

Suspension

Some of the small boys in the field
cough in their play. One
kicks the ball straight through the fence.
Along the way, a woman leans there,
taking in the winter sun. Green threads
of holiday lights hang down from the houses.
A bell rings for the children, the ball
still now in the patchy grass.

To know you not by the senses
but by the mind, I don't mind; we are
all solitaries. Day has been ending
for the entirety of day.

Compass

Occluded, the hours with you,
as we await the arrival of an answer
that is too big to voice. Should your desk
face the wall or the window? Does the mind
go there when you're not there, when you're
not working at all but travelling again,
on the ferry, on the train, in the motor
driving up to the other house.

Inroads

This is a small country, he said,
there are too many trains. And then
they get old, and things break down.
And the system is complex, and that
makes for breaks and failures.
Plants encroach on the tracks,
the land encroaches, sweet gale, cotton grass.

—

On Monday she surveyed the calendar
that tabled the hours of departure
for the first and last trains between
the three cities that sprawled together.
If I miss the connection, she said,
I can wait and have a coffee inside.
Pigeons walked platform 7 for the 08:28.

—

The moss encroached on trees, giant beech,
slender beech, old leaves encroached,
ivy and holly joined in dominion,
one birch marked itself, another
signaled from afar, leaves in ruts,
leaves in ditches, ditchwater and water
on the path that leads either

out of the forest or farther within.

Flatlands

We pull away from the center of the city,
poverty, business parks,

trashed strips of ground, tire graveyards, gasometers,
modern bungalows, swans and ducks in a canal,

tall grasses, fields and sheep

and then the always classical landscape.
The wood with its innumerable pathways.

—

Or green spreading
on the willows, mechanical shovel
on the building site beside the mixer
turning cement, fly ash, aggregate and water.

My mind begins to drift as a storm
collects over the land we've since departed,
as if danger were averted only for us,
who had boarded the train—

Everyone's asleep.

Classical Experiment

I dreamt I wrote to x around
the borders of a piece of hatched
paper he had written on; alternate
wheat and fallow, some

exhaustion land. It is said that,
after paradise, after a time,
the unfallen animals came
down the road and went

their separate ways: peacock, boar,
pheasant, rabbit; small birds roved
the fields and hedges; expanding under-
storeys of holly in woodlands;

spitting rain. Successes and lapses.
Plots halve in the drawing:
plans for second-floor passages
in the first house. Wheat begins growing.

II

Once

          In the night, the bed was as long
as the hours, the hours were as long as the road
or the future, the past was not our destiny,
the foreboding or foretelling was left
on the shelves to the longplaying records
we'd switch on for the warmth of the scratches
that pocked the music like rain, as the needle
wandered all that black circumference—

Rain Begins

My friend, one of the horsemen of the apocalypse,
can spot the others far off, "insecuring our condition."
We repair to the Seven Stars for a drink.
Members of the bar spill out with evening,

the pavement blossoming with white shirts.
Then he phones in, all smiles, and disasters
vanish, the both of us stop counting them,
and I listen, and rain begins, sends us back

to the close and noisy room, humid with beer,
where the lawyers argue away the day's
arguments and he might still show, we think.

From a Letter

In Suffolk, after Christmas, the coast
was dry. The dog went round the back
of the house and crossed the spongy field
to the river. Barked once; returned.

Angela came by to "fill up the last glass,"
she announced enigmatically. All
that was unspoken was symptom of the hours
waiting for your voice and face, our assignation.

She sat with Joe. You said "the wonder was"
your hostess had asked you to sew the Christmas goose.
You had doubled then tripled the black thread.
"What type of needle did you use?" "A goose-needle."

Increase

January rain, inordinate thunder.
The day is over over there.

A dog bays at traffic, trucks
come up the road from the bridge,
bearing heads of lettuce to the city;

rain falters, lessens; then much,
then little, then nothing;

you are asleep now, undone
in the bedclothes over there.

En Face

"As if it were a heuristic and yet cannot
be gainsaid," he said. As continuous
as thought, I thought, as rain over the surface
of the earth. Facing him at the table, I caught

the warm look of someone whose neck
I have kissed, whose ear.
To stir the white paint,
to change the dream. We'd met on the off-beat,

the time between lunch and five, and braved
the almost destroyed thing over wine and olives
in the stony basement bar on—was it
John Islip Street? John Cowslip Street?

Wintered

The long January starved the kingfishers.

–

A man brought a tray of tiny pancakes
to the crowd gathered in the vestibule.
Cherry, honey, and pepper vodka in bottles
lined up behind the bar.

–

The bore was that they kept coming upon
one another. She shone with disapproval.
He was unimpressed, repeatedly. He stepped
out of the shop into the rain
and stared at his phone, the bricks slick with leaves
and rain drumming his slicker as he walked
to his bicycle, locked to itself beside the canal.

–

The neighbors' curtains closed,
a sick child sleeping. Hammering
on the other side of the building site.
The copper dome wrapped in white tarp.
In the haul from the second-hand bookshop,
one volume falls open exactly at
"It was the winter wild,
While the heaven-born Child,"
(a black cloth edition from
R&KP, 1960s).

—

Winged fabulous creature with a human face
lying in the glass case, talisman, she longs
to slip it into her pocket and walk about with it.
Outside, geese call themselves together
near the Water Authority building.
Snow is still on the cupola,
the southern-facing windows bright as copper.

House Tour

Spinoza, lens grinder, lived here, sat
at his small wooden lathe by daylight.
The ground glass saturated his lungs
as he transmuted his materials.

The speaker calls up death, *"le fin domestique
et privé,"* and the room is colder.
Several pull their coats close.

He then postulates a miracle and moves
across the room to close the window,
dull as copper now in the failing light.

To Admit

She made a cup of tea and took up
pencil and book, reading lines aloud,
ticking the good ones. She then
smoked half a cigarette, pinched it closed,
put it back in the packet.
"It's probably a big mistake," she said
out loud, but couldn't place the remark.

—

"My bad conscience was nothing other
than terrible vanity," he said in interview.
"And I was terribly cruel. So
I don't have anything to do
with conscience now." They went
outdoors and stood by the boats
on shore, pointing at outness.

—

When the phone rang, she'd speak to her sister
for hours. "I would go so far
as to say," she would say. She watched
as neighbors from across the way
moved past their windows.
The room grew darker. "Insofar as,"
she would say. She went as far as that.

Ivor Gurney

He was a cinema pianist after the war.
The awning flapped above the patrons,
shivering, waiting for entry,
waitress bearing coffee, grey blouse

flecked with rain. Against the building,
soaked bicycles. He prepared the score indoors.
He seems to have forgotten his sleep
but waiting for him were two horses, one

with a golden saddle, one with a silver saddle,
and a mule with a leather saddle
on the far side waiting for him,
"no hole, no way to be seen."

Whorls by Bike-Lamp

It was snow on water
snow whitening the world
or vanished along the black walls
of the canal. Paint and mould.
A coot paddled towards
the discarded television.

Concertgebouw

On tram-line twenty-four, at the pivoting mid-
section, she nearly lost her balance and fell
into her neighbor's wet coat. The umbrellas
had dripped on her boots from Damrak to here.
She was on her way, though she questioned the wisdom.
Her body would not carry out instructions from
her brain. But helpless as she was, she valued
his other features, his flights, about the storied
dead musician, thanks to whom all the harpsichords
in the land were rescued from attics and barns
where they'd been unplayed by all but farm animals,
say, the chickens flying up and landing on the keys.

Asleep Awake

They pushed the old Renault 4, engine asleep
—"the donkey of the automotive species"—
a way down the dirt road till it
met the asphalt, started up again
and the shift on the dash trembled. Then
they were along the dark shore, as petals
and leaves around closed up in the dusk.

—

He reversed through the hours of the day.
He remembered all sensations since waking,
though not all feelings, which were
so many or so uniform that he
could not tell the constriction in
his chest from the jacket buttoned
around his torso in the damp car.

Disuse

Without you is within all utterance
(though I don't like to say so, nor do I
much like the word). Gone are the days
of *ultra* as far out, and *ur*
as original, or originary cry.
Nonetheless, superlatives aside,
diction is telling. I type this, late
as usual to your jokes, I lag and lag,
and surpass myself in my obsolescence.

Apartments

I counted all the shuttered windows,
all that was forbidden, the chicanery, the perilous,
it rang in my ears, all in need of renewal,
the temperature and atmosphere thick
in my lungs, spilt mercury, voluntary
breathing, unable to sleep,
afraid to take a lover for fear of putting him
in danger, though I am otherwise
a safe pair of hands. In the cinema,
the detective was involved in serious
threat-to-life investigations. The scene
of children in danger made everyone
anxious. Some of the children of the children
in each generation survived.

On. On. Stop. Stop.

In the old recording of the birthday party,
the voices of the living and the dead
instruct twelve absent friends
on the reliable luxury of gratitude.
The celebrated one hands out presents.
The dead dog barks once.
We take one another's hands and follow
their lead, past the garden wall, out to the land
still stripped by winter. Those gone
do not usurp those here. We keep
the warning close; the timbre of their voices
mingles with the sounds of traffic
going much faster to its destinations.
Is it the size or the scale of the past
on the small reels of the cassette?
Someone gives her a new pot, which,
she exclaims, is too great a luxury for her.
Someone's missing who can convert
the currencies. The old treasure
was dropped in the furrows
to await spring, with rings and pennies
and guilders and other denominations
from those pockets and fingers.

Leave

The children who dug a hole in the garden
of the house rarely visited uncovered
the limb bones, and I, lately arrived,
spoke to the parents before I called the police.
Let them play here later, I'd said.
I put the phone down. The grass
grew in patches on the ground, the oaks
rose at the edge of the property as if newly
taking possession of a lease long since expired.

Open Country

In the photograph, the two of them
sit on a bench under the apple tree
and look far out, beyond us,

at figures in the meadow—or is it
at the sun itself behind the rows of trees
(sun in the drinks on the table)

warming their clothes and faces?
Each holds a hot cigarette,
and the photo too is only a blotch

of grays and black, as if to prepare us
as well as them for the journey
to Gravesend, written on the back
of an envelope in his jacket pocket—

Photograph: Paestum, c. 1860, Anonymous

The temple of Ceres darkens
in its very columns on the swampy ground.
The tree beside it is mightier now, over all
it spreads its limbs, its leaves and creepers
seek the air for increase. All the air
is like a great hall ready to receive those sounds.
The temple on its old feet, on the way
to gravity, up-holds itself for the concert.

II to III

"Accurst, and in a cursed hour he hies."
He laid the book down, felt himself falling
short. The shortness of breath was the hour
of reckoning, set by some keeper—the keeper
of inhalations—is it common, does everyone hear
like this? He was caught. The thorns in the thicket
scored his shirt. He crouched in the dried leaves
and imagined himself elsewhere, beside her—

as if he might, for balance, take her hand—
it would be easy again, he is thinking,
wondering if he has heard it in the clear,
if he can see, clearly, what's calling
or compelling him now. "HAIL holy light."
He shifts his weight and lies down, there in the leaves.

On the Ground

i.m. Joshua Shackleton

When the collie saw the child
break from the crowd,

he gave chase, and since they both
were border-crossers,

they left this world.
We were then made of—

affronted by—silence.
The train passed Poste 5, Paris,

late arrival, no luck, no
enlarging commentary

magnified in any glass.
"The ineffable

is everywhere in language,"
the speaker had said

in the huge hall where
I sat amongst coughers,

students, in the late
February of that year,

at the end of a sinuous
inquiry on sense and sound—

"and very close to the ground," he'd said.
Like mist risen

above the feet of animals
in a far field north of here.

III

In the Corridor

I passed through, I should have paused.
There were a hundred doors.
Behind one of them, someone whose name
is not yet known to me lived out

his middle years in simple terms: two chairs,
one place laid for early breakfast, one plate
with dry toast and butter softening. There
his mind raced through writings

he had memorized long ago while he tried
to get hold of himself. Once in his youth
he had studied with love
in the corners of old paintings

grids of fields and towns,
passages intricate and particular, wheat,
columns, figures and ground,
classically proportioned

in lines that were meant
to meet, eventually,
at vanishing point. They continued,
nevertheless; they troubled the eye.

He collected sets of books printed
in the nineteenth century, unyielding
pages, memoirs of the poets,
engravings of rurified private subjects

in times of public sector unhappiness,
frescoes of human oddity in gatefold printing.
Why does it continue
to chasten me, he says to no one.

It does. It is a painful mistaking,
this setting something down,
saying aloud "It is nothing, yet"
when he'd meant, not anything—

but then nothing peered
through the keyhole, nothing
took possession. Snow on the roofs,
snow in traces on the ground,

passersby with wet trouser-cuffs
looking to the pavement as the hill rises,
light gathering in the river
and gradually spreading.

Men and Sheep

After "Mens en schaap"

Rutger Kopland (1934–2012)

Men think that we here in the distance
are a flock of sheep—let them think,

we are not of a kind, we have no words
for ourselves, we still live in a time

when men too were sheep, and only
spoke grass, read light, wrote water.

Zwijgen

I slept before a wall of books and they
calmed everything in the room, even
their contents, even me, woken
by the cold and thrill, and *still*
they said, like the Dutch verb for falling
silent that English has no accommodation for
in the attics and rafters of its intimacies.

Cover

Nettle, thistle, dandelion, clover
by the dry stone wall. Light, then clouds,
then light, conversant with the seemly structure
of thinking, and the stops. Warmth of the bench.
You inside saying to someone, "I like
that." Rain begins to know the table.

Milk Street

We're done with unpromising tasks.
The hours between us a hand's brevity,

breviary in hand, with only grass for binding,
and levity, and misery, their felicities.

Summered

Bales of hay stacked like modernist houses
in the neighbor's field. Window on the turn,

a new stem of the creeper fingering it.
He closed it and closed his eyes.

Calm of the lime-plaster wall.
Damp stone scent of the corner

never visited. He sat at the table
soaked in sunlight, mail stacked

by the typewriter in the as-yet
unspent hour. The old animal troughs

filled with shoes and bent rackets, yellow
rubber gloves folded over

a white bucket, Morandi's
objects herded together

on a postcard
next to a jar of pencils.

—

He eats a sandwich at one
and circles the rooms
of the house. Opens the door,

leans his hip on the jamb.
Protagonist of
late summer, marsh swallow,

rib and spine or
rafter and beam.

—

A dog watches its master
sweep the road. The white panicles
of buddleia bending. Foxgloves
reseeding themselves.

—

On the one hand, I could ask you
a question. On the other, could I
ask you a question?

We enumerate the gains and losses,
spanning for gold. Soft mouth beside me,
lips not on me, though we both think of it.

—

They were burning the old ling
in the dream. All those fields
of bell heather, fen violet,
milk violet. He held

some blackberries in his
cupped hand. I put one
in my mouth, when it rolled
on my tongue a bee turned.

—

"There are seasons of complete failure on the moors, such as 19—, 19—, 19—, and 19—, when many bee colonies . . . were lost from starvation. I well recall going round the stances of many northern beekeepers during August 19— . . . and finding the ground in front of the hives carpeted with crawling dying bees. Milk churns filled with sugar syrup were taken to the moors, and wherever possible the crawling bees were swept up on to shovels and dumped into the tops of nearby hives, then lightly sprayed with syrup. After an hour or so, when there was some response from the bees and they were gently humming, the old type of round feeders were put on every hive. . . . Eventually, among those colonies that had not died out, a small amount of heather honey was stored in the brood combs. . . . And with further heavy feeding upon their return home, some of these stocks of bees managed to survive the dreadful winter . . . of 19—.

It would appear that hours of sunshine play an important part in the equation when the colonies are on the moors."

Colin Weightman on the moorland apiaries

i.m. Nikel Lambrechtsen

An Essay on Total Colony Collapse

A bee hovers over the lip and crawls again
into the foxglove. And the meadow reaches all the way
to the hill, to the forest at its borders, to us awaiting
the captains of thousands and the captains of hundreds,
their honey and their care, to keep them
away from echoing rocks and the smell
of the clay, and to seek instruction
from the gods when they vanish away.

An Essay on Perspective

I wanted to read an essay in his wrist.
The afternoon was endless. Out the window,
a lane to the right bent away,
taking with it the figure moving down it.
Alone for a quarter of an hour,
looking in, plotting the argument,
that benefit of rhetoric, there arrived
the true but unlikely moment—

only one of us has to make a move
for our troubles to be told and halved.

Eaves

The hillside in the rain—
standing under the eaves,

rows of collapsing boots,
litter of firewood, overturned boxes—

the falling steady then intermittent,
distinct, undivided, and how vast

the ornamental green flag of the field.
And then, one sudden rush down—

as if the whole of the air, light and the damp
scent of it, turns its face to us.

Field Experiments

*Between 1843 and 1856, Lawes and Gilbert started nine
long-term field experiments, of which they abandoned only
one, in 1878 . . . They are the oldest, continuous agronomic
experiments in the world.*
　　　　—Rothamsted Long-term Experiments (2006)

　　　　　　　　. . . and what will thrive and rise
　　and what the genius of the soil denies.
　　　　—Dryden

Crows wading in the grass.

　　–

Sleeping like one struck down.
Sleeping like one murdered.

　　–

Dogs follow the procession of tractors.
Last birds. First moths.

Creatures of the recessional hours.

　　–

I joined the line of cleaners on the lawn,
collecting plastic cups, sandwich packaging—

Indoors, collapsed shelves,
heaps of books, plaster dust, chunks of mortar—

–

In the library, scent of orange peel
on the hands of the reader beside me.

As he types, I type. And as
it can only be this close,

that is, we can be only
as close as this, I must try

not to think of his fingers
at all. A member of staff

strides by. Two books
lie on their faces on the table.

–

"It was his own Jacobean
revenge tragedy disguised
as a publisher's meeting.
At the end I felt lightly brushed
by the wing of insanity."

–

The donkey's ears turn delicately
separately in their pins as the cars pass

while inside the thicket of thorn and willow, a hop.

–

Pigeons settling, unsettling in nerves of flight.

–

We are on the outer wheel of knowing.
They are on the inner wheel. They'd say,
though they have no strength to say,
it doesn't help. In ten days,
we, too, will be on the inner wheel.

–

Night and rain.

–

Deaths in the past, and in the future?
death there would come upon us faster
than we could make meaning of it.

—

Just visible to her, beyond the bed, the tops of trees
where wild parakeets settle on Christmas morning.

—

So what was admitted?

—

In the experiment, on discrete strips of land,
permission for any grass that traveled there,
in any of these forms (from the dictionary):
to receive, to let in, to grant access to,
to accept, to listen to, to permit,
sanction, endure. And it is tolerable
to be compatible with, to incur,
to commit, to perpetrate, to let go, release,
to acknowledge (as true).

—

                    To breathe
all of this. Rain ongoing, unattended
by wind on a failing afternoon. Inside,
three women sort grass seeds.

—

Heavy smell of summer in the trees.
The Oxford Book of Fugitives stands on the shelf
in the shuttered house. Such sleep and peril
in the caution. The cautious student of lust
reads and sleeps and does not hear the voices
that ring in her ears, why wake to regret
in the warning, buoyant regret.

—

It moves to the knuckles and fingers.
It moves to the bones of the face.
And dulls. And days begin.
A span of secular holidays?
And yet, were no trace left, I'd know it.
Wouldn't I? I've known it
from its first entrance in.
"Love," you said (of Herbert,
was it?), "is always
a step ahead of you."

—

Pushing off, the bicycle frame ticking
and shuddering, the wheels crushing sand
on the path down along the woods, the fields,
beeches and birch, mainverb, corn or
barley or grass, or pasture on approach,
beyond, within, receding.

—

The visitor passes by on tip-toe—
in one room a mother and infant
asleep in the summer's afternoon,
and down the hall, behind another door,
a student cleans and readies his oboe,
wetting a reed once cut by the god of fields.

—

"Go to the psalm, look there
for the cornerstone," the historian
on the radio said. "Go to the classical
rhetoricians," the other one said, "look there
for signs of the true Jacobean
question mark." Blind metal radio.
You, the *fil electrique exposé*,
irresolute on the sofa,
while we, wrecked, loose-leaf assemblages
of persons as I touch your knee.

Faring

A door opened on another room,
its own were ajar, white doors,
a figure removing into the shadow,

I thought I should call your name,
or learn what names you were called,
bearer of joists, bearer of metaphor,

you turning to the left, or the bereft,
the light nervous and uncertain
through the leaves of the birch,

the light precision of your glance,
luminous on the white surfaces
in the enfilade of chambers,

mansions, in the unmeasured number
of meanings in sheltered and opened spaces,
in the sound of the rain,

should I ever learn your true name
I should know the house, the floor, the windows,
the doors before which I was allowed

to stand, as if ajar myself,
as if opened despite
where we were or were not to go—

Night-Jar

Hawking for moths at the close
early hour. The clouded browns of the feathers
read as shadow only above damp ground, or as
memory, and then, against the dark
easterly light of the trees, it has gone—
somewhere inside the edges.

After *Gewritu secgað*

from The Exeter Book

It is written in scriptures that this
creature appears plainly to us
when the hour calls,
while its singular power compels
and confounds our knowing.
It seeks us out, one by one,
following its own way; fares on,
with its stranger's step, never
there a second night, native
to no place; moves according
to its nature. It has no hands,
no feet, has never touched the ground,
no mouth to speak of,
nor mind. Scriptures say
it is the least of anything made.
It has no soul, no life, but travels
widely among us in this world;
no blood nor bone, but
consoles all the children of men.
It hasn't reached heaven,
it won't touch hell,
but takes instruction from
the king of glory. The whole story
of its fate—limbless as it is,
animate—is too obscure to tell.
And yet all the words we find
to describe it are just and true.
If you can say it, call it
by its rightful name.

Notes & Acknowledgments

"Night-Jar": For Charles Donker.

"Night-Jar," "Classical Experiment," "Increase," and "To Admit" were first published in *Joining Music with Reason: 34 Poets, British and American, Oxford 2004–2009*, edited by Christopher Ricks (Chipping Norton, Oxforshire [UK]: Waywiser Press, 2010).

"Increase": "then much, then little, then nothing" is from Samuel Beckett's *Texts for Nothing, 9*, for which (and much else) thanks to Catherine Barnett.

"Men and Sheep": Rutger Kopland's *"Mens en Schaap"* appeared in his collection *Geduldig gereedschap* (Amsterdam: Van Oorschot, 1993); this translation (with thanks to Claar Hugenholtz, Geertruid van Wassenaer, Arent van Wassenaer, and Just Wiarda for help and clarifications) was first published in *The Palm Beach Effect: Reflections on Michael Hofmann*, edited by André Naffis-Sahely and Julian Stannard (London: CB Editions, 2013). I am grateful to Uitgeverij G.A. van Oorschot for permission to publish the translation.

"Summered": The quotation by Colin Weightman is from his pamphlet *Heather Honey* (Hebden Bridge [UK]: Northern Bee Books), pp. 6–7, a revised and expanded chapter from his book *The Border Bees: Anecdotes and Memoirs of Twenty Years, 1940–1960* (Consett, County Durham [UK]: Ramsden Williams Publications, 1961).

"After *Gewritu secgað*": First published in *The Word Exchange: Anglo-Saxon Poems in Translation,* edited by Greg Delanty and Michael Matto (New York: W. W. Norton & Co., 2010).

Thanks to the editors of the following journals, in which some of the other poems first appeared: *Battersea Review, Blackbox Manifold, The Chicago Review, Electronic Poetry Review, The Louisville Review, Poem-A-Day, Poetry, The White Review,* and *The Wolf.*

Thanks also to the Wiarda and Hamilton families; Nick Hornby and Ben Folds, and Charlie McDonnell; Bashir Abu-Manneh, Daniel and Olivia Brush, Miranda Field, Linda Gregg, Janna Israel, Paul Keegan, Nick Laird, Joanna Picciotto, John Ryle, Meg Tyler, and Fiona Wilson; and the graces.

I am deeply grateful to the John Simon Guggenheim Memorial Foundation and the National Endowment for the Arts for grants that allowed me to complete this work.

SASKIA HAMILTON is the author of two previous poetry collections, *As for Dream* and *Divide These,* and a selection of her poems, *Canal,* published in Britain. She is the editor of *The Letters of Robert Lowell,* and co-editor of *Words in Air: The Complete Correspondence between Elizabeth Bishop and Robert Lowell.* She teaches at Barnard College and lives in New York.

The text of *Corridor* is set in Albertina MT. The font was completed in 1965 by Chris Brand, who was a teacher of design and typography and known for book cover designs. The first use of this font was in 1966 by the Albertina Library in Brussels for an exhibition catalogue of Stanley Morison's work. Book design by Rachel Holscher. Composition by BookMobile Design & Digital Publisher Services, Minneapolis, Minnesota. Manufactured by Versa Press on acid-free, 30 percent postconsumer wastepaper.